PIÑATA
Party

NORTHERN PLAINS
PUBLIC LIBRARY
Ault, Colorado

Kitiya
Palaskas

CONTENTS

For Finn and Bella

Happy crafting!

Introduction

So it seems you have found my little piñata book. How exciting!

I've been making piñatas for many years and, in my opinion, they're the ultimate party accessory. There's just so much to love! Not only do they look super fancy and instantly make a party more festive, but they're also stuffed to the brim with treats — and everyone loves a treat. Also, smashing them is a great way to release all those pent up pre-party nerves — just don't miss and hit the guests!

My work as a craft-based designer focuses on mastering traditional handmade techniques and re-imagining them in contemporary ways. I've always been so inspired by Mexican culture, in particular its art and craft. I've also always loved a good party, so re-creating the piñata — such an iconic and festive object — in my own style has been an amazing and fun thing to try as part of my design practice.

Once you've mastered my basic technique, you'll be whipping up piñatas in no time, and most of the materials you'll need are easy to find at your local art or craft store. Most of the piñata projects in this book will need a template, which you can find on pages 106–109. You'll also need access to a photocopier to enlarge the templates. So clear your schedule, grab some snacks (no one likes a hangry crafter) and set yourself up for an epic good time, because I'm about to take you on a fun, fringe-filled adventure.

Kitiya x

Piñata essentials

Here is a list of the basic tools and materials
you'll need to create the piñatas in this book.

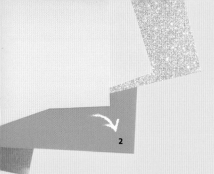

7 SCORING TOOL

You can find these in the scrapbooking section of most art or craft stores. If you can't find one you could always use an empty ball-point pen.

1 PLAIN CARD

Look in art stores for screenboard: 76 x 102 cm (30 x 40 in) sheets, 620 gsm, 1 mm (1⁄16 in) thick. If you can't find screenboard, any lightweight cardboard at this size and thickness will work.

2 ASSORTED CARD

Usually around 240–250 gsm; available in a range of sheet sizes, colours and treatments (such as glitter and metallic). Some projects ask for a 'large sheet of card': the sheets I use for these projects measure around 50 x 63 cm (20 x 25 in).

3 CREPE PAPER

4 TISSUE PAPER

5 SCISSORS

Two types: a basic pair for cutting paper plus pinking shears.

6 CUTTING KNIFE AND CUTTING MAT

These are not strictly necessary, but you may prefer to cut out shapes with a cutting knife instead of scissors.

8 MASKING TAPE

9 DOUBLE-SIDED TAPE

10 PENCIL

11 RULER

12 HOLE PUNCH

I use a single-hole scrapbooking punch, but a regular two-hole punch will also work. For some projects, you may find it easier to use a screwdriver to punch the holes.

13 HOT-GLUE GUN

A small hand-held glue gun with refillable glue sticks.

14 CORD

For hanging the piñatas; I use cord about 3 mm (1⁄8 in) thick.

15 SCREWDRIVER

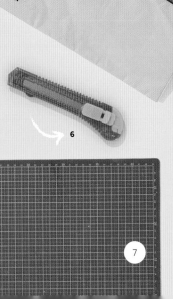

A crash course in piñata construction

If you've ever made a piñata using traditional papier-mâché techniques, you'll be able to appreciate the time and dedication it takes to create one, not to mention the amount of sticky paste needed to build that baby up. While I've enjoyed my fair share of gloopy good times constructing piñatas the old-school way, I've designed all the projects in this book to be made without the need for papier-mâché at all. Not only is the technique way less messy, but you'll be able to build a piñata in a relatively short period of time, which is perfect for when you need to pimp up your party décor at the last minute.

This section will skill you up on the basic papercraft construction technique used to create most of the piñatas in this book. Read it well my friends, because you'll be referring back to it often. Anything that deviates from this method will be described in full within the project itself, so don't worry, I've got you covered.

Basic piñata construction

The majority of the piñatas in this book are designed to look 2D while being a 3D form. They're comprised of a front and back panel, and a thin side panel strip that joins the front and back together. This strip wraps all the way around the side of the piñata. A hanging cord is attached, and a little section is left open at the top so you can fill your piñatas with treats and then seal it closed. You'll be using crepe paper to make fringing to decorate your piñatas, with some of the finer details being cut from coloured card and attached to the piñata using a hot-glue gun.

YOU WILL NEED

Piñata template (these are located on pages 106–109)

Scissors

Pencil

Ruler

Screenboard (card stock)

Hole punch

Masking tape

Scoring tool

Cord for hanging

Treats for filling

Crepe paper

Double-sided tape

FOR SOME PROJECTS YOU MAY ALSO NEED:

Coloured card

Hot-glue gun

▶ STEP 1

Use a photocopier to enlarge and print the template to size. Cut out your template and trace around it onto the screenboard. You'll need to trace two templates: one for the front and one for the back panels of your piñata. In all the projects I'll refer to this step as 'transferring the template onto screenboard'. Cut out the two shapes.

▶ STEP 2

Cut a long strip of screenboard, 10 cm (4 in) wide. The length of this strip will vary depending on the project (I'll let you know how long each time). This strip will form the side panel of your piñata. Sometimes you'll need an extra long strip, so you will have to stick two pieces of screenboard together.

▶ STEP 3

Place the front and back panels together, then use a hole punch or screwdriver to punch a hole through both panels, near the top of the shape. You'll use these holes for attaching the hanging cord.

▶ STEP 4

To stick the side panel (the long strip of card) to the first panel (either the front or back), start at the top of the shape and, with the side strip flush along the panel edge, attach the two using short strips of masking tape at regular intervals.

▶ STEP 5

There will be occasions where the piñata shapes have corners or indents. It's important to make sure the side panel strip folds neatly around or into these areas to get a perfect piñata shape. While you are sticking your side edge to the first panel, affix it all the way up to the corner or indent, then flip the piñata onto the side edge, so the strip is flat on the table. Then, use a ruler and the scoring tool to score a line across the side panel strip at the exact position of the corner or indent. Fold the strip so it wraps around the piñata snugly.

If you're like me and you love your piñata too much and can't bear to smash it and see your handiwork destroyed before your very eyes, you can bypass the candy filling bit (step 8) and make your piñata a decorative piece instead.

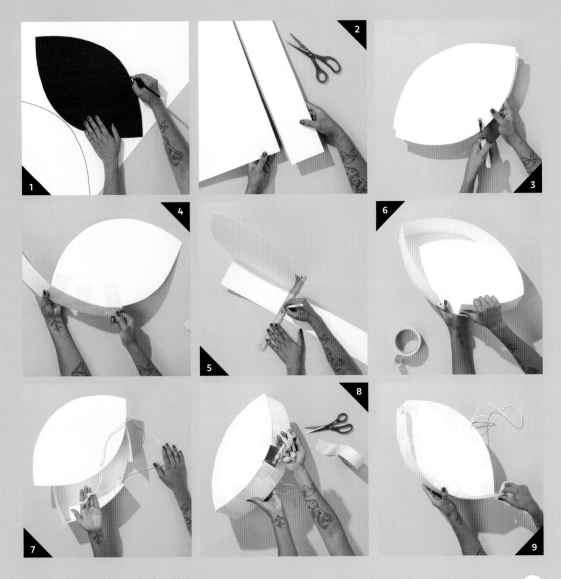

▶ STEP 6

To create a hole for the piñata fillings, you'll need to leave a gap in the side panel. In each project I'll give you an indication of how long your side panel strips need to be, which will account for this gap, but if you're filling your piñata with larger pieces of candy or trinkets, you'll need to trim any excess side panel that's in the way. Make sure the hole is always at the top of the piñata.

▶ STEP 7

Thread a length of cord through the holes. Tie off the cord inside the piñata to conceal the knot. You will need to do this before you stick the second panel on.

▶ STEP 8

Complete the piñata construction by sticking the second panel on in the same way you affixed the first one. Once this is done, fill your piñata with treats, then seal the hole with a few layers of masking tape. If you want the piñata to be extra secure, you could even cut a rectangular piece of card that fits over the candy hole and stick that on with masking tape.

▶ STEP 9

For extra durability, reinforce the outer edges of the piñata with a long strip of masking tape. You might want to do this twice if you're filling the piñata with heavy stuff so it doesn't break prematurely, because that would be a total vibe kill.

Making the piñata fringe

In each project I have listed the crepe paper amounts by the packet. These quantities are only approximations, and you'll probably have leftovers each time, so you might want to start a piñata supplies stash. This will minimise waste and build up a collection of pre-cut fringe in a variety of colours that you can use for future projects.

▶ STEP 1

To create fringe for your piñata, cut a segment from the folded crepe paper packet, about 3 cm (1¼ in) wide.

▶ STEP 2

Take the folded segment and find the middle. Insert your scissors into the middle and cut up the fold line, leaving about 1 cm (½ in) uncut at the top. Repeat this step on the other end of the segment. Close up the segment so it's flat again.

▶ STEP 3

Make cuts all the way along the length of the segment, on the same side as your first two cuts. Space each cut about 5 mm (¼ in) apart, leaving the same 1 cm (½ in) uncut along the top of the strip. Once

you've done this, ruffle the cut edge to separate the individual crepe paper sheets, as they can fuse together when you're cutting through multiple layers. Gently unfold each layer to reveal your fringe.

MINI FRINGE

To make mini fringe for small piñata projects, simply cut the crepe paper segment at a smaller width — try 2 cm (¾ in) — and make your cuts closer together. Some projects ask for 'tiny, finely cut' fringe, which is a bit smaller again. You may need to make these cuts layer by layer, as it gets fiddly and messy trying to cut through multiple layers of crepe at close intervals.

Covering the piñata

Decorating the piñata is my favourite part of the process, because it brings the project together and makes everything look lush and perfect. If your piñata looks like a hot mess after you've slapped masking tape all over it, don't sweat it! The piñata fringe will hide all your sins.

▶ STEP 1

Affix double-sided tape onto the front and back faces of the piñata, from top to bottom, spacing the lines of tape about 2 cm (¾ in) apart. In the same way, affix double-sided tape across the side edge panel, all the way around the piñata, 2 cm (¾ in) apart. To avoid the fringe falling down on the underside or base of your piñata, affix the strips of tape closer together, or even flush against each other, so the fringe has more to stick to.

▶ STEP 2

Starting on the front and back panels, attach the crepe paper fringe in rows, working from bottom to top, attaching the fringe perpendicular to the rows of tape. To achieve a flatter, more minimal look, overlap each row by 2 cm (¾ in).

For a fuller coverage, overlap each row by 3 cm (1¼ in). Don't worry if your rows get a bit wonky; it will add character.

▶ STEP 3

After you've covered one panel, trim the fringe to fit the curve of the piñata. You might need to clean your scissors with eucalyptus oil on a cloth, as they can get clogged up with residue from the double-sided tape.

▶ STEP 4

Attach the fringe around the side panel, then trim to fit the piñata curve.

▶ STEP 5

For some projects, you'll need to cut out decorative details from coloured card. Attach them to the piñata using a hot-glue gun.

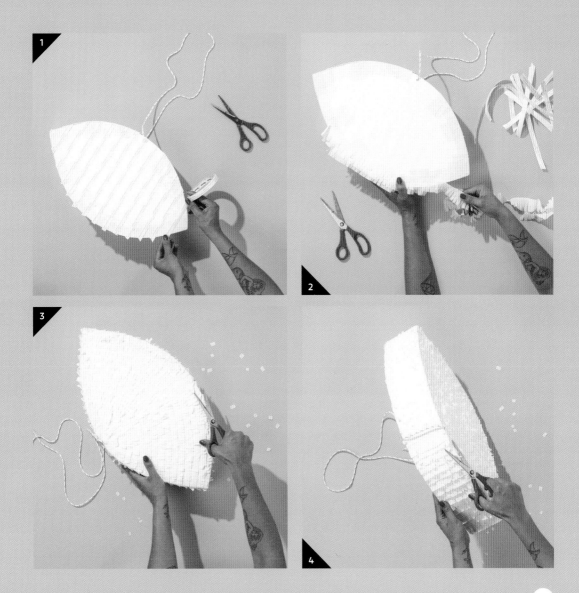

SNACK TIME

I love snacks so much! I'm often happier with a plate full of assorted bits and pieces than with a full meal: a boiled egg, a leftover slice of pizza, a sneaky slice of cake on the run... These projects are for people (like me) who love to eat. Which is basically everyone, right?

Pizza slice piñata

When we were teenagers, my best friend Kelly and I had an after-school routine of ordering a family-sized cheese pizza (with added corn!) and then pigging out while watching our favourite movie (Empire Records) on repeat. Years later, I still love pizza, but tragically I also seem to have developed a gluten allergy, so I guess this is my way of getting my pizza fix without the bloat.

YOU WILL NEED

Pizza slice template (page 106)
Scissors
Pencil
Ruler
1 sheet screenboard: 76 x 102 cm (30 x 40 in), 620 gsm
Long strip of screenboard for side panel: 10 x 164 cm (4 x 64½ in)
Hole punch

Masking tape
Scoring tool
Cord for hanging
Treats for filling
Crepe paper: 1 packet yellow, ¼ packet orange
Double-sided tape
Coloured card for pizza toppings
Hot-glue gun

How to make a
Pizza slice piñata

▶ **STEP 1**

Using a photocopier, enlarge the
pizza slice template by 830 per cent.
Following step 1 on page 10, transfer
the template onto the screenboard and
cut out two pizza slices.

▶ **STEP 2**

Following the instructions on pages
10–12, assemble the piñata using the
two pizza slices and the side panel strip.
Attach the hanging cord. Fill the piñata
with treats and seal.

▶ **STEP 3**

Following the instructions on page 13,
create fringe for the piñata using
yellow crepe paper for the cheese
and orange for the crust.

▶ **STEP 4**

Following the instructions on pages
14–15, apply double-sided tape to both
faces and the side panel of the piñata.
Cover the piñata with yellow fringe,
starting at the pointy end of the pizza
slice and following a slight curve as you
move up towards the top edge. About
10 cm (4 in) from the top, switch to
orange crepe paper for the crust.

▶ **STEP 5**

Create a variety of pizza toppings in
your favourite flavour combos using the
coloured card, then attach to both sides
of the pizza slice using a hot-glue gun.

Bacon and egg piñatas

My friend Dan laughs at me sometimes because I have this weird habit of boiling an egg to eat on the go, which then ends up rolling around loose in the bottom of my handbag, or in a jacket pocket – a tragically forgotten snack. I originally wanted to make a boiled egg piñata – so that every time I look at this book it will remind me that there's probably an egg in my pocket – but I thought a fried egg would look better. And seeing as you can't have eggs without bacon, here's the pair.

YOU WILL NEED

Bacon and egg templates (page 106)

Scissors

Pencil

Ruler

2 sheets screenboard: 76 x 102 cm (30 x 40 in), 620 gsm

2 long strips of screenboard for side panels: 10 x 136 cm (4 x 53½ in) for the egg, 10 x 145 cm (4 x 57 in) for the bacon

Hole punch

Masking tape

Scoring tool

Cord for hanging

Treats for filling

Crepe paper: 1 packet white, ½ packet yellow, 1 packet red

Double-sided tape

Coloured card: pink, white

Hot-glue gun

▶ STEP 1

Using a photocopier, enlarge both the bacon and egg templates by 830 per cent. Following step 1 on page 10, transfer the templates onto the screenboard and cut out two bacon shapes and two egg shapes.

▶ STEP 2

Following the instructions on pages 10–12, assemble both piñatas using the bacon and egg shapes and the two side panel strips. Attach the hanging cords. Fill the piñatas with treats and seal.

▶ STEP 3

Following the instructions on pages 13–15, create fringe for the piñatas using white crepe paper for the egg, yellow crepe for the yolk and red for the bacon. Apply double-sided tape to both faces and the side panel of each piñata, then cover the piñatas with fringe.

▶ STEP 4

To decorate the bacon piñata, cut a variety of wiggly shapes from the pink and white cards. Affix these shapes to both sides using the hot-glue gun.

Chicken drumstick piñata

Designing food-themed piñatas seems to have become a way for me to indulge my food cravings without any consequences, so I thought it essential to include something in this book that honours my ultimate food kryptonite: fried chicken.

YOU WILL NEED

Chicken drumstick template
  (page 106)

Scissors

Pencil

Ruler

1 sheet screenboard: 76 x 102 cm
  (30 x 40 in), 620 gsm

Long strip of screenboard for side
  panel: 10 x 152 cm (4 x 60 in)

Hole punch

Masking tape

Scoring tool

Cord for hanging

Treats for filling

Crepe paper: 1½ packets gold,
  ¼ packet white

Double-sided tape

How to make a Chicken drumstick piñata

▶ **STEP 1**

Using a photocopier, enlarge the chicken drumstick template by 830 per cent. Following step 1 on page 10, transfer the template onto the screenboard and cut out two chicken drumstick shapes.

▶ **STEP 2**

Following the instructions on pages 10–12, assemble the piñata using the two drumstick shapes and the side panel strip. Attach the hanging cord. Fill the piñata with treats and seal.

▶ **STEP 3**

Following the instructions on page 13, create fringe for the piñata using gold crepe paper for the chicken and white for the chicken bone.

▶ **STEP 4**

Following the instructions on pages 14–15, apply double-sided tape to both faces and the side panel of the piñata. Cover the piñata with gold fringe, starting from the large curved base. When you've covered up to the chicken bone in gold, switch to white fringe.

Cake slice treat box

On the night that I moved out of home I ate a huge, elaborately decorated piece of cake for dinner. It was such a novelty that I could have dessert for any meal, without anyone telling me what I should or shouldn't eat — even now, I still think that's the best thing about being an adult! This project reminds me of my first taste of independence.

If you like, go crazy and make a bunch of these treat boxes to form a whole cake, which would look awesome as a party centrepiece.

YOU WILL NEED

Cake slice template (page 107)

Scissors

Pencil

Ruler

1 sheet screenboard, 76 x 102 cm (30 x 40 in), 620 gsm

Strip of screenboard for side panel: 10 x 50 cm (4 x 19¾ in)

Masking tape

Scoring tool

Treats for filling

Crepe paper: ¼ packet mint green, ¼ packet white

Double-sided tape

Pinking shears

Assorted coloured card for cake fillings and toppings

Hot-glue gun

Ready-made pompom for decorating (optional)

How to make a Cake slice treat box

▶ STEP 1

Using a photocopier, enlarge the cake slice template by 313 per cent. Following step 1 on page 10, transfer the template onto the screenboard and cut out two cake slices. (You will have some leftover screenboard, but you can save this for another piñata project.)

▶ STEP 2

Following the instructions on pages 10–12, assemble the piñata using the two cake slices and the side panel strip. Leave the pointy end of one of the triangular panels unstuck so you can fill the box with treats. As this is a treat box, you won't need to attach a hanging cord. Fill the box with treats and seal.

▶ STEP 3

Following the instructions on pages 13–15, create mini fringe for the piñata using mint green crepe paper for the top and back of the cake slice, and white for the rest. Apply double-sided tape to both faces and the side panel of the piñata. Cover the piñata with fringe.

▶ STEP 4

Use scissors and pinking shears to cut some strips of coloured card and use the hot-glue gun to affix them around the two white side panels of the cake slice. Cut out tiny strips of card and glue them on top of the cake. If you like, glue a small pompom on top.

Liquorice allsorts party prop

I once went to a costume party dressed as a pink liquorice allsort. It was kind of impractical and looked like I wasn't wearing any pants, but I loved it anyway. Here I've re-created this costume in fringed form. While this project makes a fun, oversized prop to use for party photos, you can still fill it and use it as a piñata, too.

The instructions given here are to make the large pink and green liquorice allsort. If you like, make a collection of them in different colours and sizes; just reduce the template size to create smaller versions.

FOR THE LARGEST LIQUORICE ALLSORT, YOU WILL NEED

6 pieces of screenboard,
45 cm (18 in) square

Scissors

Masking tape

Crepe paper: 1½ packets pink,
1½ packets green, ½ packet black,
½ packet white

Double-sided tape

How to make a Liquorice allsort party prop

▶ STEP 1

Place one square of screenboard on a large, flat surface (I like to work on the floor for big projects). To create the sides of your liquorice allsorts cube, line up four of the other cardboard pieces along each edge of this square, laying them flat on the floor. Apply masking tape along the edges of the central square, to join it to the other four squares. Flip the whole thing over and apply masking tape along the same edges on the back side.

▶ STEP 2

To construct the cube, fold up the four sides and stick masking tape down the vertical sides to form an open cube shape. Apply masking tape to the inside edges of your cube for extra durability.

▶ STEP 3

Place the last square on top of the open cube and tape along each edge to seal.

▶ STEP 4

Following the instructions on pages 13–15, create fringe for the piñata using pink and green crepe paper for the top and bottom parts of the liquorice allsort, and black and white for the stripes in the middle. Apply double-sided tape to all six sides of the cube and cover each side with fringe.

To turn this prop into a piñata, simply use a hole punch or screwdriver to poke two holes along the top of one of the sides, spacing the holes 5 cm (2 in) apart. Thread a hanging cord through the holes and knot it. Fill the cube with treats before sealing it with the remaining cardboard square.

TOOLS OF THE TRADE

I couldn't make a craft book without paying homage to the objects I use on a daily basis to create my work. Whether I'm scribbling ideas in my notebook, colouring in or cutting and pasting, you'll always find at least one of these tools on my desk.

Scissors piñata

In the world of craft-based design, my scissors are my best friend. This piñata would make a great gift for that creative mate you know, who (like me) can't live without a trusty pair of scissors by their side.

YOU WILL NEED

Scissors template (page 107)

Scissors

Pencil

Ruler

1 sheet screenboard: 76 x 102 cm (30 x 40 in), 620 gsm

Long strip of screenboard for side panel: 10 x 314 cm (4 x 123¾ in)

2 shorter strips of screenboard for holes inside scissor handles: 10 x 36 cm (4 x 14¼ in)

Hole punch

Masking tape

Scoring tool

Cord for hanging

Treats for filling

Crepe paper: 1 packet silver, 1 packet red

Double-sided tape

Hot-glue gun

2 blue card circles, 5 cm (2 in) in diameter

NORTHERN PLAINS
PUBLIC LIBRARY
Ault, Colorado

How to make a Scissors piñata

STEP 1

Using a photocopier, enlarge the scissors template by 830 per cent. Following step 1 on page 10, transfer the template onto the screenboard and cut out two scissors shapes.

STEP 2

Following the instructions on pages 10–12, assemble the piñata using the two scissors shapes, the side panel strip and the two shorter side panel strips. Attach the hanging cord. Fill the piñata with treats and seal.

STEP 3

Following the instructions on page 13, create fringe for the piñata using silver crepe paper for the scissor blades and red for the handles.

STEP 4

Following the instructions on pages 14–15, apply double-sided tape to both faces and the side panel of the piñata. Cover the piñata with silver fringe, starting from the pointy end of the blades. When you've reached the handles, switch to red fringe.

STEP 5

To finish, use the hot-glue gun to affix a blue card circle to each side, on the blades, just above the handles.

This is one of the more complicated projects and it may get a little messy. Take your time with it and don't worry: the piñata fringe will hide all your sins.

Sticky tape piñata

One of my biggest stationery-related gripes is being in the middle of a crucial task that requires immediate adhesion, reaching over and not being able to find the end of the sticky tape. So annoying, right? So, to the person who invented the tape dispenser, I salute you.

YOU WILL NEED

Sticky tape template (page 107)

Scissors

Pencil

Ruler

1 sheet screenboard: 76 x 102 cm (30 x 40 in), 620 gsm

Long strip of screenboard for side panel: 10 x 187 cm (4 x 73¾ in)

Hole punch

Masking tape

Scoring tool

Cord for hanging

Treats for filling

Crepe paper: 1 packet light blue, ½ packet pale yellow

Double-sided tape

Assorted coloured card for details: purple, orange, pink

Hot-glue gun

How to make a
Sticky tape piñata

▶ STEP 1

Using a photocopier, enlarge the
sticky tape template by 830 per cent.
Following step 1 on page 10, transfer
the template onto the screenboard
and cut out two sticky tape shapes.

▶ STEP 2

Following the instructions on pages
10–12, assemble the piñata using the
two shapes and the side panel strip.
Attach the hanging cord. Fill the piñata
with treats and seal.

▶ STEP 3

Following the instructions on pages
13–15, create fringe for the piñata using
light blue crepe paper for the tape
dispenser and pale yellow for the sticky
tape roll. Apply double-sided tape to
both faces and the side panel of the
piñata. Cover the piñata with fringe.

▶ STEP 4

Cut two sets of long, thin strips from
the purple and orange cards. Cut two
larger circles from the purple card and
two slightly smaller circles from the
pink card. Using the photo as a guide
for placement, stick these shapes onto
each side of the piñata using the hot-
glue gun.

▶ STEP 5

Cut a piece of pale yellow crepe paper
and attach it to the top of the piñata,
imitating a strip of tape.

Pencil piñata

This is one of my favourite projects in this book, because I'm one of those people who are super obsessed with oversized versions of things (as well as super tiny versions of things). It strays from the standard piñata-making technique into more 3D territory, so I think you'll have fun with it.

YOU WILL NEED

Pencil templates: pencil body, pencil
    base (page 108)

Scissors

Pencil

2 sheets screenboard: 76 x 102 cm
    (30 x 40 in), 620 gsm

Ruler

Scoring tool

Hole punch

Cord for hanging

Masking tape

Treats for filling

Crepe paper: 1 packet yellow,
    ½ packet cream, ¼ packet pink,
    ¼ packet silver

Double-sided tape

1 black card circle, 11 cm (4¼ in)
    in diameter

Pinking shears (optional)

Hot-glue gun

6 strips black card: 4 x 34 cm
    (1½ x 13½ in)

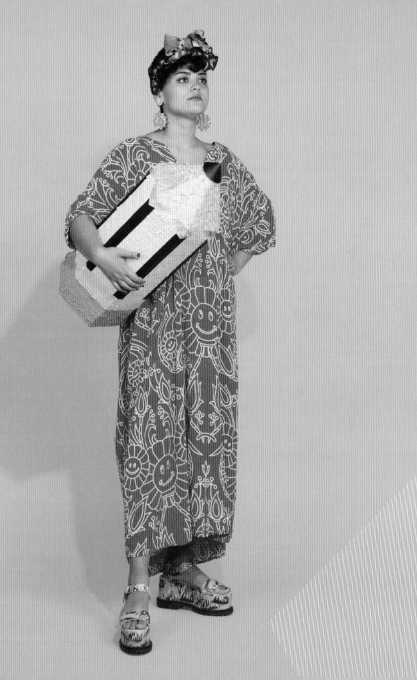

How to make a Pencil piñata

▶ STEP 1

Using a photocopier, enlarge both pencil templates by 830 per cent. Following step 1 on page 10, transfer the templates onto the screenboard (save the leftover board for another project). While the template for the pencil body is still on top of your board, use the ruler and scoring tool to score over all the fold lines. Cut out the two shapes.

▶ STEP 2

Punch two holes in one of the outer edges of the main pencil body, spacing the holes about 5 cm (2 in) apart. Thread the cord through the holes and knot it. To create the body of the pencil, fold the pencil body component into shape. Seal all edges with masking tape.

▶ STEP 3

Fill the piñata with treats. Tape the pencil base to the bottom of the piñata.

▶ STEP 4

Following the instructions on pages 13–15, create fringe for the piñata using yellow crepe paper for the main body of the pencil, cream for the top, and pink and silver for the eraser part. Apply double-sided tape to all panels of the pencil, then cover with fringe.

▶ STEP 5

To make the lead tip, take the black card circle and cut a zigzag edge around the circle (if you have them, use pinking shears to do this). Make a cut in the card, from the edge to the centre point. Shape the circle into a cone, then overlap and secure the edges with hot glue. Glue the lead to the tip of your pencil.

▶ STEP 6

Fold the strips of black card in half lengthways and glue them onto each edge of the pencil, as shown in the photo.

Crayon treat boxes

The smell of crayons is one of my earliest memories. I love these treat boxes because you can make them in all sorts of colours to match the rest of your party décor. When it's party time, pull the cord like a party popper to burst the treat box open.

The instructions given here are to make one treat box in red; I've also made a yellow and blue one, but you can make as many as you like.

FOR ONE TREAT BOX, YOU WILL NEED

1 red card circle, 8 cm (3¼ in) in diameter

Pencil

Ruler

Scissors

Toilet paper roll

Hot-glue gun

Treats for filling

1 small red card circle, the same diameter as the toilet roll

Thin cord, 12 cm (4¾ in) in length

Assorted coloured card for the crayon details: purple, black, white

Pinking shears

⅛ packet red crepe paper

Double-sided tape

How to make a Crayon treat box

▶ STEP 1

To make the crayon tip, take the red card circle and make a cut in the card, from the edge to the centre point. Shape the circle into a cone shape that fits the diameter of the toilet roll, then overlap the edges and secure with hot glue.

▶ STEP 2

Glue the cone onto one end of the toilet roll using hot glue. Fill with treats.

▶ STEP 3

Use a pencil to poke a small hole in the centre of the small red card circle. To create a pull cord, tie a knot in the cord and thread it through the hole. Cut out a small circle from purple card and trim the edge with pinking shears. Attach the circle to the end of the pull cord using hot glue.

▶ STEP 4

To close the treat box, squeeze a thin line of hot glue around the open base of the toilet roll, then affix the small red card circle to the glue, with the knot on the inside.

▶ STEP 5

Following the instructions on pages 13–15, create mini fringe for the piñata using red crepe paper. Apply double-sided tape to the toilet roll, then cover the piñata with fringe, making sure the fringe covers any stray glue.

▶ STEP 6

Using the photo as a guide, cut some decorative shapes from the black and white card. Affix these in place with hot glue.

Mini piñata pencil topper

I really wanted to include a traditional Mexican piñata in this book, so here it is in the cutest mini form, as a pencil topper. Make a whole bunch of these and put them in treat bags as party favours.

YOU WILL NEED

Small polystyrene ball, 5 cm (2 in) in diameter

Blue acrylic paint

Paintbrush

Pencil

Scissors

7 small segments of crepe paper in assorted colours, 3 x 5 cm (1¼ x 2 in)

7 small segments of white crepe paper, 3 x 5 cm (1¼ x 2 in)

Hot-glue gun

7 semicircles in assorted coloured card, 5 cm (2 in) in diameter

How to make a Mini piñata pencil topper

▶ STEP 1

Paint the polystyrene ball with blue paint and set it aside to dry. Once completely dry, poke a hole in the ball using the base of a pencil.

▶ STEP 2

Following the instructions on page 13, create mini fringe using the 14 crepe paper segments.

▶ STEP 3

Using the hot-glue gun and the seven coloured fringes, scrunch or roll up one of the fringe segments and glue it onto the middle of the straight edge of each semicircle, with the fringe facing away from the curved edge of the semicircle.

▶ STEP 4

Take the two corners of the semicircle and fold them inwards to form a small cone (like a mini party hat). Secure with dabs of hot glue. The fringe should now be sticking out from the point of the cone. Repeat with the remaining six fringes and card semicircles.

▶ STEP 5

Use the hot-glue gun to affix the cones evenly around the polystyrene ball.

▶ STEP 6

Trim the remaining seven white fringe segments along the long edge down to 2 cm (¾ in), then glue one segment around the base of each cone.

▶ STEP 7

To finish the pencil topper, squeeze a dab of hot glue onto the end of the pencil, then push the pencil into the hole you created in the ball.

Mini ruler streamers

This is the easiest and quickest project in this book, so treat yo'self and give it a whirl.

Cut strips of white paper, 2 x 15 cm (¾ x 6 in) in size. Use a red pen to draw ruler markings and measurements along both sides of the strip. Twist each end in opposite directions to curl the paper slightly. Make a whole bunch of these and use them as piñata fillings.

FOREVER SUMMER

If I had to epitomise myself in a book chapter, this would be it. I only ever feel truly myself when the sun is shining and I'm swizzling some sort of insane tiki cocktail on a beach, with 'Temperature' by Sean Paul playing on the radio. Here is everything you need to keep those tropi-vibes alive all year round.

Palm tree hanging decoration

Hang this shiny guy over your tropical snack table, turn on 'Coco Jambo' by Mr President with the sound on full, and get that party started!

I found the popcorn buckets at my local hospitality/catering supply store, but you can also order them online. For a smaller decoration, use coffee cups instead of popcorn cups and decrease the percentage of your palm leaf enlargement in proportion to the cups.

YOU WILL NEED

Palm leaf template (page 108)
Scissors
Pencil
4 large sheets metallic green card
Screwdriver
14 round cardboard popcorn cups:
   mine were 11 cm (4¼ in) in diameter
   and 18 cm (7 in) high

3½ packets gold crepe paper
Double-sided tape
Cord for hanging, 2 m (80 in)
   in length
Hot-glue gun
Green tissue paper

How to make a
Palm tree hanging decoration

▶ STEP 1

Using a photocopier, enlarge the palm leaf template by 830 per cent. Following step 1 on page 10, transfer the template onto the green metallic card and cut out six palm leaves. Fold each leaf in half lengthways to make a crease down the centre, then unfold.

▶ STEP 2

Use the screwdriver to poke a small hole in the centre of the base of each popcorn cup.

▶ STEP 3

Following the instructions on pages 13–15, create fringe for the tree trunk using gold crepe paper. Apply double-sided tape to each cup, then cover with fringe.

▶ STEP 4

Tie a knot at the end of the cord, then thread the cord through the hole in one of the cups, with the cup's open end facing down, so the knot is hidden inside the cup. Make another knot in the cord, 4 cm (1½ in) above the first cup, then thread a second cup on. You want the cups to overlap slightly. Continue this process until all cups are threaded onto the cord.

▶ STEP 5

Use the hot-glue gun to stick the leaves onto the base of the last cup. Arrange the leaves all the way around the base and then mould the leaves gently so they curve down and over the trunk slightly. If the leaves are flopping over too much, prop them up by gluing scrunched-up balls of green tissue to the underside of each leaf.

Pineapple piñata

This project was the first piñata I ever designed and made, so it's a special one because it really kicked off this whole thing for me. If you're the kind of person who will eat pineapple pieces until your tongue burns off, and can't go past a piña colada without taking a sip, then a) you are my soul mate, and b) this project is for you.

YOU WILL NEED

Pineapple templates: curved side panel, circle, small and large pineapple leaves (page 106)

Scissors

Pencil

1 sheet screenboard: 76 x 102 cm (30 x 40 in), 620 gsm

Ruler

Scoring tool

1 large sheet green card

Hot-glue gun

Masking tape

Hole punch

Cord for hanging

Treats for filling

Double-sided tape

1 packet yellow crepe paper

How to make a Pineapple piñata

▶ STEP 1

Using a photocopier, enlarge the curved side panel template by 830 per cent. Following step 1 on page 10, transfer the template onto the screenboard and cut out two side panels. Use the ruler and scoring tool to score a line on each piece, where it tapers at one of the short ends. Fold along this line.

▶ STEP 2

Enlarge the circle template by 830 per cent. Transfer the template onto the screenboard and cut out two circles.

▶ STEP 3

Enlarge the leaf templates by 830 per cent. Transfer onto green card and cut out five small and five large triangles. Fold each triangle in half lengthways to make a crease down the centre, and at the fold lines indicated on the templates.

▶ STEP 4

Shape each curved side panel into an open cone, overlapping the edges to the fold line, then use hot glue to join the ends together. Secure with masking tape.

▶ STEP 5

To attach the cord, take one of the cones and punch two holes opposite each other, near the top of the smaller opening. Thread the cord through the holes and tie in a knot.

▶ STEP 6

To create the shape of the pineapple, place the two open cones together, with the larger open ends facing each other. Tape the two cones together.

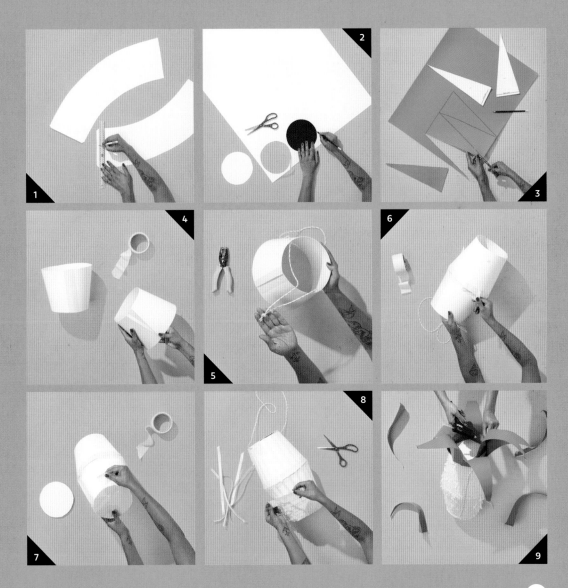

How to make a
Pineapple piñata (CONTINUED)

▶ STEP 7

Tape one screenboard circle to the base of the piñata (the end without the cord). Fill the piñata with treats, then attach the second circle to the top of the piñata.

▶ STEP 8

Following the instructions on pages 13–15, create fringe for the piñata using yellow crepe paper. Apply double-sided tape to the piñata and cover in yellow fringe, leaving the top circle uncovered.

▶ STEP 9

Make a small cut up the centre of each triangle leaf, cutting into the base of the triangle and up to the fold line, creating two tabs. With the triangles slightly folded along the fold line and with the tabs overlapping and facing inwards, glue each leaf onto the top of the piñata (the end with the cord). Start with the smaller triangles in a ring around the outside of the top, then the larger ones within that.
To shape the leaves, curve them down over the edge of the piñata and curl the tips around a pencil.

Tropical cocktail piñata

You can't have a tiki bar without a classic cocktail, and you can't have a classic cocktail without all the trimmings. Fancy straws, swizzle sticks, paper umbrellas and a fruity garnish are my must-haves. You can impress your guests by switching up the colours and trimmings of this piñata to match the drinks at your party. This project is one of the more involved of the bunch, so keep it chill and don't rush it. You could even mix yourself a drink while you work. In fact, I insist.

YOU WILL NEED

2 sheets screenboard: 76 x 102 cm (30 x 40 in), 620 gsm

Masking tape

Scissors

Ruler

Pencil

Hot-glue gun

Hole punch

Cord for hanging

Treats for filling

2 large pieces of card for umbrella stand and straw

Crepe paper: ⅛ packet pink, ⅛ packet red, ⅛ packet dark blue, ⅛ packet white, 1½ packets teal, ½ packet mint green, ⅛ packet orange

Double-sided tape

Orange card for fruit decoration

How to make a
Tropical cocktail piñata

STEP 1

To form the cocktail glass, shape one piece of screenboard into a loose cone-like shape with two open ends, one larger than the other. Secure the cone along the overlapped edges using masking tape. Use scissors to trim the top and bottom of the cone edges so they are even.

STEP 2

Measure the diameter of the smaller opening of the cone, then draw a circle on the remaining piece of screenboard, approximately 6 cm (2½ in) wider than the opening. Cut out the circle and glue it over the smaller opening of the cone.

STEP 3

To attach the hanging cord, punch two holes opposite each other, near the top of the open end. Thread the cord through the holes and tie in a knot.

STEP 4

Cut a circle from screenboard to fit the larger opening of the cone. Cut two holes in the circle, about 3 cm (1¼ in) and 4.5 cm (1¾ in) in diameter. Attach the circle to the opening using masking tape. Fill the piñata with treats through the holes. Reinforce the entire piñata along all edges using masking tape.

STEP 5

To make the umbrella and straw, roll two large pieces of card into tubes to fit the holes at the top of the piñata. The umbrella tube will insert through the smaller hole and the straw through the larger hole. Secure with masking tape. Cut a circle from screenboard, 30 cm (12 in) in diameter. Following the instructions on page 62 (Fringed cocktail umbrella), fold the circle into an umbrella shape. Glue the umbrella onto the narrower cardboard tube.

How to make a Tropical cocktail piñata (CONTINUED)

▶ **STEP 6**

Following the instructions on pages 13–15, create fringe for the umbrella using pink and red crepe paper. Create fringe for the straw using blue and white crepe paper. Apply double-sided tape to the umbrella and straw and cover with fringe. Leave a portion of the umbrella stand uncovered, so you can slot it into the top of the piñata.

▶ **STEP 7**

Create fringe for the cocktail glass using teal and mint green crepe paper. Apply double-sided tape to the glass and cover it entirely in fringe, using mint green for the top and base of the glass, and teal for the middle.

▶ **STEP 8**

To make a decorative orange fruit slice, cut out a circle from screenboard about 23 cm (9 in) in diameter. Cut out a quarter of this circle and discard. Cut out a thin circle from orange card and

glue it around the edge of the fruit slice. Using the photo as a guide, lightly draw four segments on each side of the circle. Create mini fringe using orange crepe paper. Apply double-sided tape to the segments on both sides of the fruit slice and cover with fringe.

▶ **STEP 9**

To complete the piñata, slot the umbrella and straw into the holes at the top of the cocktail glass and secure with dabs of hot glue. Glue the orange fruit slice to the side of the glass.

For drawing circles, I usually draw around an object with a similar diameter, such as a cup or small plate. Alternatively, you can use a drawing compass if you prefer.

Fringed cocktail umbrella

Even though store-bought cocktail umbrellas are super cute, there's a huge novelty about making your own from scratch. Here's how.

Draw a circle onto a piece of screenboard, 8 cm (3¼ in) in diameter, then cut it out. Locate the centre of the circle, then draw a line from the centre to the edge. Cut along this line, then fold the circle into a wide cone shape and secure the overlapping edges with a few dabs of hot glue.

Following the instructions on pages 13–15, create mini fringe for the umbrella using crepe paper. Apply double-sided tape to the top of the umbrella and cover with fringe. Use hot glue to stick a short wooden skewer onto the underside of the umbrella.

Fruit slice straw decoration

There are so many amazing decorative straws on the market these days, but more is more in my opinion, so why not take it up a notch by adding these cute fruit slices?

Draw a circle onto a piece of screenboard, 8 cm (3¼ in) in diameter, then cut it out. Cut the circle in half. Using the photo as a guide, lightly draw three triangles on one side of the semicircle, to resemble the segments of a fruit slice.

Following the instructions on pages 13–15, create tiny, finely cut fringe from yellow crepe paper. Apply double-sided tape to the fruit segments and cover with fringe. Use a strip of colourful washi tape to attach the straw to the back of the fruit slice.

Repeat these steps in orange and lime green to create a citrus collection.

Tiki party invitation

If you can't quite find the time to carve your own tiki head out of a tree log (next time maybe), this could be a good back up. Your guests will love receiving these unique invitations, then pulling the cord to reveal a confetti surprise, and the details of your party.

FOR ONE INVITATION, YOU WILL NEED

Toilet paper roll

Hot-glue gun

2 brown card circles, the same diameter as the toilet roll

Printed party details

Confetti (ready-made or see page 104)

Pencil

Thin cord, 12 cm (4¾ in) long

⅛ packet brown crepe paper

Scissors

Double-sided tape

Tiki face template (page 109)

Small pieces light brown card for the face details (I used two tones of brown)

How to make a
Tiki party invitation

~~~~~~

▶ **STEP 1**

Using the toilet paper roll and the hot-glue gun, glue one brown card circle to one end of the roll. Create a hard copy or digital design of your party details and print it out. Put it inside the roll, along with some confetti.

▶ **STEP 2**

Use a pencil to poke a small hole in the centre of the remaining brown card circle. To create a pull cord, tie a knot in the cord and thread the cord through the hole. To close the invitation, squeeze a thin line of hot glue around the open base of the toilet roll, then affix the card circle to the glue, with the knot on the inside.

▶ **STEP 3**

Following the instructions on pages 13–15, create tiny, finely cut fringe using brown crepe paper. Apply double-sided

tape to the toilet roll, then cover with fringe, making sure the fringe covers any stray glue.

▶ **STEP 4**

Using a photocopier, enlarge the tiki invite template by 254 per cent. Following step 1 on page 10, transfer the template onto the brown card and cut out each piece. Use the hot-glue gun to stick the face details onto the fringe-covered roll, with the pull cord end at the bottom of the face.

▶ **STEP 5**

Cut a decorative shape from the remaining brown card and glue it to the end of the pull cord. To reveal the details of your party, guests can pull the cord like a party popper to burst the invite open.

GOOD VIBES

I'm so inspired by the iconography and motifs found in graphic art, interior design, and homewares from the 1970s. The vivid colour palettes and bold, playful silhouettes evoke such fun, fancy-free feelings. These playful piñatas pay homage to this unique moment in design history.

Rollerskate piñata

When I was a kid I was in a rollerskating club, and have recently got back on the skates to relearn the ways. In my mind's eye I think I look like a graceful swan but, in reality, I spend most of the time just fumbling and falling over. Ah well, at least this rollerskate piñata is flawless!

YOU WILL NEED

Rollerskate template (page 107)

Scissors

Pencil

Ruler

1 sheet screenboard: 76 x 102 cm (30 x 40 in), 620 gsm

Long strip of screenboard for side panel: 15 x 220 cm (6 x 86¾ in)

Hole punch

Masking tape

Scoring tool

Cord for hanging

Treats for filling

Crepe paper: 2 packets white, ⅛ packet dark blue, ⅛ packet violet, ⅛ packet yellow, ½ packet magenta

Double-sided tape

Thin pink ribbon: 6 x 17 cm (6½ in) lengths; 1 x 30 cm (12 in) length

Hot-glue gun

4 yellow card circles, 7 cm (2¾ in) in diameter

How to make a Rollerskate piñata

STEP 1

Using a photocopier, enlarge the rollerskate template by 830 per cent. Following step 1 on page 10, transfer the template onto the screenboard and cut out two shapes.

STEP 2

Following the instructions on pages 10–12, assemble the piñata using the two rollerskate shapes and the side panel strip. Attach the hanging cord. Fill the piñata with treats and seal.

STEP 3

Following the instructions on pages 13–15, create fringe for the piñata. Use white crepe paper for the main part of the rollerskate, dark blue and violet for the stripes up the side, yellow for the brakes on the front, and magenta for the wheels. Apply double-sided tape to the entire piñata and cover with fringe.

STEP 4

To create shoelaces for the rollerskate, tie a knot in each end of the six lengths of 17 cm (6½ in) pink ribbon. Apply hot glue to each knot and attach pairs of these ribbons in a cross formation up the side panel (the front of the skate), folding the ribbon over the knot so it's hidden from view. Tie the 30 cm (12 in) length of ribbon into a bow and glue it to the top of the laces.

STEP 5

Glue the four yellow card circles to the centre of the wheels.

Mushroom piñata

One of my favourite things about 70s design is the use of unusual colour combos to create a trippy vibe. Pair that with a mushie motif and you've got yourself a pretty psychedelic party decoration.

YOU WILL NEED

Mushroom template (page 108)

Scissors

Pencil

Ruler

1 sheet screenboard: 76 x 102 cm (30 x 40 in), 620 gsm

Long strip of screenboard for side panel: 10 x 159 cm (4 x 62½ in)

Hole punch

Masking tape

Scoring tool

Cord for hanging

Treats for filling

Crepe paper: 1 packet magenta, ½ packet red

Double-sided tape

1 x A3 sheet orange card

Hot-glue gun

How to make a Mushroom piñata

▶ STEP 1

Using a photocopier, enlarge the mushroom template by 830 per cent. Following step 1 on page 10, transfer the template onto the screenboard and cut out two mushroom shapes.

▶ STEP 2

Following the instructions on pages 10–12, assemble the piñata using the two mushroom shapes and the side panel strip. Attach the hanging cord. Fill the piñata with treats and seal.

▶ STEP 3

Following the instructions on pages 13–15, create fringe for the piñata using magenta crepe paper for the mushroom cap and red for the base. Apply double-sided tape to the entire piñata and cover it with fringe.

▶ STEP 4

Cut out circles from the orange card and affix them to the mushroom cap using hot glue.

Rainbow piñata

There's something so joyous about a rainbow. It's so rare and magical to see one in the sky, but I feel like I'm always missing them because I spend a lot of time indoors at my desk. Here's a way to bring the rainbow inside so you can enjoy it all the time.

YOU WILL NEED

Rainbow template (page 108)

Scissors

Pencil

Ruler

1 sheet screenboard: 76 x 102 cm (30 x 40 in), 620 gsm

Long strip of screenboard for side panel: 10 x 172 cm (4 x 67¾ in)

Hole punch

Masking tape

Scoring tool

Cord for hanging

Treats for filling

Crepe paper: ¼ packet blue, ¼ packet green, ¼ packet yellow, ¼ packet orange, ½ packet red

Double-sided tape

How to make a Rainbow piñata

▶ STEP 1

Using a photocopier, enlarge the rainbow template by 830 per cent. Following step 1 on page 10, transfer the template onto the screenboard and cut out two rainbow shapes.

▶ STEP 2

Following the instructions on pages 10–12, assemble the piñata using the two rainbow shapes and the side panel strip. Attach the hanging cord. Fill the piñata with treats and seal.

▶ STEP 3

Following the instructions on pages 13–15, create fringe for the piñata. Apply double-sided tape to the entire piñata and cover it with fringe. Start with the blue layer first, then move up to green, yellow, orange and finally red, curving the fringe as you stick it on, to follow the curve of the rainbow.

Fringed hanging decoration

Inspired by a dreamcatcher, this majestic decoration would make an amazing centrepiece hung over a party table, freeing up space on the tabletop for party food or presents. You could also make mini versions and hang them from the backs of chairs, on door knobs, or strung in multiples as a garland.

YOU WILL NEED

Peace sign template (page 109)
Scissors
Pencil
Ruler
1 sheet screenboard: 76 x 102 cm (30 x 40 in), 620 gsm
Hole punch

Pink cord for hanging, plus extra cord, 90 cm (35 in) in length
2 packets light purple crepe paper
Double-sided tape
Tissue paper in assorted colours
10 thin coloured cords, about 13 cm (5 in) in length

How to make a Fringed hanging decoration

▶ STEP 1

Using a photocopier, enlarge the peace sign template by 830 per cent. Following step 1 on page 10, transfer the template onto the screenboard and cut it out.

▶ STEP 2

Use the hole punch to make a hole at the top and bottom of the peace sign. Attach the pink hanging cord to the top hole and the extra length of cord to the bottom.

▶ STEP 3

Following the instructions on pages 13–15, create fringe for the peace sign using purple crepe paper. Apply double-sided tape to the entire sign (front and back) and cover it with fringe.

▶ STEP 4

Using tissue paper and following the instructions for making tassels on page 105, make ten tassels in assorted colours. Use the thin coloured cord to tie the tassels onto the pink cord at the bottom of the sign, positioning them down the length of the cord.

Flower power cake toppers

Cake toppers are a clever way to decorate without using fancy frosting techniques and are also great at hiding icing crimes, which I tend to commit regularly when baking. The flower shapes were inspired by motifs found on my collection of retro towels and bedsheets — they always have the best prints!

YOU WILL NEED

Floral cake topper templates
  (page 109)

Scissors

Pencil

Thin card in assorted colours

Hot-glue gun

Wooden skewers

Small segments of crepe paper
  in assorted colours

Double-sided tape

How to make the Flower power cake toppers

▶ STEP 1

Using a photocopier, enlarge the three floral cake topper templates by 483 per cent. Following step 1 on page 10, transfer the templates onto the assorted coloured card. You will need two of the same flower shape for each topper. It's up to you how many flower cake toppers you make.

▶ STEP 2

Cut out small circles from the coloured card to fit into the centre of each flower. Use the hot-glue gun to affix these shapes to the flowers.

▶ STEP 3

Glue two of the same flower shapes together, with the decorated sides facing out, and sandwiching a wooden skewer in between. Repeat for the remaining flowers.

▶ STEP 4

Following the instructions on pages 13–15, create mini fringe for the flower stems using assorted coloured crepe paper. Cut 30 cm (12 in) strips of fringe. Apply double-sided tape around each skewer. Wrap the fringe around the skewers, leaving at least 6 cm (2½ in) uncovered at the bottom of the skewer, to stick into the cake.

BLACK MAGIC

Fun fact: I used to be a teenage goth. I know this may be hard to believe, given the amount of colour in this book, but it's true. My dark, fishnet-clad world was filled with mystical things such as tarot cards, ouija boards, magic spells and crystals that I charged by the light of the full moon while listening to Cradle of Filth as I sat inside a candlelit pentagram. Ah, such fun-filled, light-hearted times. Let's relive our teen goth days by making these piñatas!

Crystal ball piñata

Put on your finest crushed velvet cloak, surround yourself with crystals and light up that smudge stick, it's time to see what the future holds! This piñata is made using a store-bought paper lampshade, which is an easy, no-fuss way to make a sphere without using papier-mâché.

YOU WILL NEED

Round paper lampshade
Cord for hanging
Pencil
Ruler
1 large sheet gold metallic card
Scissors
Hot-glue gun

Treats for filling
Plain tissue paper
Masking tape
2 packets purple metallic crepe paper
Double-sided tape
Silver glitter card

How to make a Crystal ball piñata

▶ **STEP 1**

Assemble the lampshade following the instructions on the packet. Tie the hanging cord at the top, attaching it to the wire frame.

▶ **STEP 2**

Draw a circle onto the metallic card that is big enough to cover the hole at the bottom of the lampshade. Cut out the circle and use the hot-glue gun to stick the circle onto the lamp base. Fill the piñata from the top with lightweight treats.

▶ **STEP 3**

Scrunch up a few sheets of tissue paper to form a long tube shape (long enough to wrap around the hole at the base), then wrap masking tape around this tube, covering the tissue completely. Bend the tube into a circular shape and secure into a ring using masking tape.

Glue this ring to the base of the piñata, around the card circle base.

▶ **STEP 4**

Cut a strip of gold metallic card, 10 cm (4 in) wide and long enough to wrap around the base of the lampshade. Glue the metallic strip around the base, to cover the paper ring.

▶ **STEP 5**

Following the instructions on pages 13–15, create fringe for the piñata using purple metallic crepe paper. Apply double-sided tape to the lampshade and cover it entirely in fringe.

▶ **STEP 6**

Using the photo as a guide, draw and cut out two starburst shapes (one large and one small) from silver glitter card. Stick them onto the piñata using hot glue.

Evil eye piñata

In many cultures, eye-shaped talismans are worn to ward off evil and protect the wearer from harm. My mum wore one throughout my childhood, so it's a very familiar and comforting icon for me. I'm not sure if this piñata is going to ward off anything, but I like to think it'll keep bad vibes from messing with your party!

YOU WILL NEED

Evil eye template (page 107)

Scissors

Pencil

Ruler

1 sheet screenboard: 76 x 102 cm (30 x 40 in), 620 gsm

Long strip of screenboard for side panel: 10 x 112 cm (4 x 44 in)

Hole punch

Masking tape

Scoring tool

Cord for hanging

Treats for filling

Crepe paper: 1 packet white, ⅛ packet metallic blue, ⅛ packet silver

Double-sided tape

How to make an Evil eye piñata

▶ STEP 1

Using a photocopier, enlarge the
evil eye template by 830 per cent.
Following step 1 on page 10, transfer
the template onto the screenboard
and cut out two eye shapes.

▶ STEP 2

Following the instructions on pages
10–12, assemble the piñata using the
two eye shapes and the side panel strip.
Attach the hanging cord. Fill the piñata
with treats and seal.

▶ STEP 3

Following the instructions on page 13,
create fringe for the piñata using white
crepe paper for the main part of the
eye, metallic blue for the iris and silver
for the pupil.

▶ STEP 4

Following the instructions on pages
14–15, apply double-sided tape to the
entire piñata and cover it with fringe.
To create the shape of the iris and pupil,
curve the fringe into a spiral as you are
attaching it, starting from the outer
edge and moving in towards the centre
of the circle.

Crescent moon piñata

There's nothing more mystical than the moon. With its many powerful properties, it packs a punch in the world of magic. And it makes a really pretty piñata.

YOU WILL NEED

Moon and star templates (page 109)

Scissors

Pencil

Ruler

1 sheet screenboard: 76 x 102 cm (30 x 40 in), 620 gsm

1 small sheet glitter card

Long strip of screenboard for side panel: 10 x 198 cm (4 x 78 in)

Hole punch

Masking tape

Scoring tool

Cord for hanging

Treats for filling

3 packets silver crepe paper

Double-sided tape

Hot-glue gun

How to make a Crescent moon piñata

► STEP 1

Using a photocopier, enlarge the moon template by 830 per cent. Following step 1 on page 10, transfer the template onto the screenboard and cut out two moon shapes. Using a photocopier, enlarge the star by 830 per cent. Transfer the template onto the glitter card and cut out two star shapes.

► STEP 2

Following the instructions on pages 10–12, assemble the piñata using the two moon shapes and the side panel strip. Attach the hanging cord. Fill the piñata with treats and seal.

► STEP 3

Following the instructions on pages 13–15, create fringe for the moon piñata using silver crepe paper. Apply double-sided tape to the entire piñata and cover it with fringe.

► STEP 4

Use the hot-glue gun to attach a glitter star onto the front and back faces of the moon.

Crystal piñatas

When I was a kid I spent all my pocket money on crystals and, to be honest, nothing has really changed now that I'm an adult. There are two different crystal templates for this project. I encourage you to make a whole collection of them in different colours and sizes because they make the most beautiful and majestic party decorations.

YOU WILL NEED

Crystal templates (page 109)

Scissors

Pencil

1 sheet screenboard (fits 2 crystals): 76 x 102 cm (30 x 40 in), 620 gsm

Ruler

Scoring tool

Hole punch

2 cords for hanging

Masking tape

Treats for filling

Metallic crepe paper: ¾ packet green, ¾ packet magenta

Double-sided tape

How to make the Crystal piñatas

STEP 1

Using a photocopier, enlarge each crystal template by 830 per cent. Following step 1 on page 10, transfer the templates onto the screenboard, making sure you also transfer the fold lines and hole punch markings (use the scoring tool to trace over these markings). Cut out the crystal shapes.

STEP 2

Use the ruler and scoring tool to score along all fold lines. Use the hole punch to make holes at the marked positions on each crystal shape.

STEP 3

Knot each cord into a loop for hanging and thread it through the punched holes on each crystal.

STEP 4

Close the crystals using masking tape along the open edges to seal. Before you close the last panel, fill each crystal with treats.

STEP 5

Following the instructions on pages 13–15, create fringe for the piñatas using a different metallic crepe paper for each one. Apply double-sided tape to the faces of each crystal and cover with fringe, trimming the edges neatly after each panel is covered.

Fringed party hats

I love a good party hat! Wearing one always makes me feel silly and playful, which is, in my opinion, the exact way you should feel at a party. These hats are made extra festive with the addition of metallic fringe and a mystical charm on top. To save time you could also use store-bought party hats, but I've provided a template so you can use it for future parties, to make hats in any pattern or colour you like.

TO MAKE TWO HATS, YOU WILL NEED

Party hat template (page 107)

Scissors

Pencil

2 x A3 sheets white card

Hole punch

Double-sided tape

Masking tape

Elastic

¼ packet metallic crepe paper (a different colour for each hat)

2 small pieces glitter card (a different colour for each hat)

Hot-glue gun

How to make the Fringed party hats

▶ **STEP 1**

Using a photocopier, enlarge the party hat template by 830 per cent. Following step 1 on page 10, transfer the template onto the white card, making sure you also transfer the hole punch markings. Cut out two party hats. Use the hole punch to create holes at the marked points on each hat.

▶ **STEP 2**

Stick a strip of double-sided tape along one straight edge of each hat. Curve each hat into a cone shape and stick together along the taped edge. Secure along this edge with a strip of masking tape on the inside and outside of the hat.

▶ **STEP 3**

Measure and cut a piece of elastic (long enough to securely hold the hat on your head). Thread the elastic through the punched holes and tie with double knots. Repeat for the second hat.

▶ **STEP 4**

Following the instructions on pages 13–15, create fringe for the hats using metallic crepe paper. Apply double-sided tape to each hat and cover with the fringe.

▶ **STEP 5**

Draw and cut out two moon and two star shapes from glitter card. Use the hot-glue gun to stick each shape together, blank sides facing in, so they are double-sided. Glue the shapes onto the top of the hats.

Fringed photo backdrop

DIY photo booths are such a great addition to a party and this epic backdrop with its luxe texture and shine will look fantastic in photos. To keep the good times going, set up a tripod with a phone holder attachment so guests can take their own shots with the automatic timer. You can make this backdrop as wide or tall as you like — just add more sheets of screenboard.

YOU WILL NEED

Masking tape
2 sheets screenboard: 76 x 102 cm
(30 x 40 in), 620 gsm
Hole punch
4 pieces of cord for hanging,
each 90 cm (35½ in) long

Scissors
8 packets gold crepe paper
Double-sided tape

How to make a
Fringed photo backdrop

▶ STEP 1

Using masking tape, attach the two sheets of screenboard together, joining them along the long edge.

▶ STEP 2

Use a hole punch to make four evenly spaced holes across one long edge (the top of the backdrop). Thread a cord through each hole and knot the ends together to form large hanging loops.

▶ STEP 3

Following the instructions on pages 13–15, create fringe for the backdrop using gold crepe paper. Cover the front of the rectangle in fringe, using double-sided tape to affix each strip of fringe. Apply the fringe in sections, changing the angle of each section to create variation and texture.

Disco ball earrings

Here's a piñata-themed project that you can wear! I love statement earrings, and have been designing and making them for a few years now. Part disco, part crystal ball, these shimmery, eccentric lil' numbers will make your party outfit pop.

YOU WILL NEED

Jewellery pliers
2 earring hooks
2 metal eyepins
Hot-glue gun

2 small polystyrene balls,
  5 cm (2 in) in diameter
Scissors
Small quantity gold crepe paper

How to make the Disco ball earrings

Following the instructions on page 13

▶ **STEP 1**

Use the jewellery pliers to attach an earring hook to each eyepin. Squeeze a dab of hot glue onto the end of each eyepin and stick one into each of the polystyrene balls.

▶ **STEP 2**

Cut out two small circles from the gold crepe paper, about 2.5 cm (1 in) in diameter. Using the hot-glue gun, stick a circle onto the base of each ball, using your hands to mould and stick the paper around the base of the ball.

▶ **STEP 3**

Following the instructions on page 13, create tiny, finely cut fringe for the earrings using the gold crepe paper.

▶ **STEP 4**

Starting from the base (where you glued the crepe paper circle) and working towards the top, carefully wrap the fringe around each ball, securing it in place with hot glue. When you have covered the ball, trim any excess fringe.

Piñata extras

No piñata experience is complete without the trimmings: smashing sticks, blindfolds, confetti and embellishments. Here's a bunch of quick and easy projects that you can make to accompany your piñatas; just change the colours and styles to match your party theme.

SMASHING STICK

Following the instructions on page 13, create fringe using crepe paper in assorted colours. Use a hot-glue gun to stick the fringe onto an old broom handle or thick dowel rod, wrapping the fringe in rows of different colours.

CONFETTI

Craft stores stock scrapbooking hole punches in every shape and size imaginable, so why not pick one that matches your piñata or party theme and punch your own confetti using coloured paper or tissue? You could also hand-cut the confetti from strips of paper or tissue, in a more free-form sort of way.

STREAMERS

Use a ruler and scalpel to slice thin 20 cm (8 in) strips of coloured paper or tissue in colours that match your party theme. To curl the streamers, use your hands to twist each end in opposite directions, or do that fancy present bow thing your mum used to do when gift wrapping, by gently dragging a scissor blade along the strip so it curls up.

MASK

It wouldn't be an authentic piñata-smashing experience without a blindfold or mask. To make one, enlarge the template on page 107 by 285 per cent and transfer onto plain card. Use a hole punch to make a hole on either end. Create mini fringe following the instructions on page 13, then affix it to the mask using double-sided tape. Attach elastic or cord to tie the mask on.

TASSELS

Tassels can make for a fancy extra touch to your piñata. Attach them to the hanging cord, or cascading from the base of the piñata on an extra piece of string. To make a tassel, cut 20 thin strips from tissue paper, each 40 cm (16 in) in length. Cut a piece of cord, 20 cm (8 in) in length. With the tissue strips laid out in a bundle, pinch them together in the centre and twist to create a twisted centre section, about 6 cm (2½ in) long. Fold the bundle in half, with the twisted section at the top and tie into a tassel using the cord, knotting it below the twisted section. Trim the tassel to your desired length.

CANDY

No piñata is complete without a candy surprise. When you're choosing your sweet fillings, I'd recommend using wrapped candy only. You don't want your sugary treats covered in gross stuff when they explode onto the ground. Not yum.

TOYS

It could be fun to include little toys in your filling selection. What you choose is up to you — just avoid anything with super sharp or pointy bits, in case something goes rogue during the smashing process and flies at someone's face. Total vibe kill! If you're stuck for ideas, most party stores sell selections of colourful, lightweight trinkets that are perfect for filling piñatas or treat boxes.

Templates

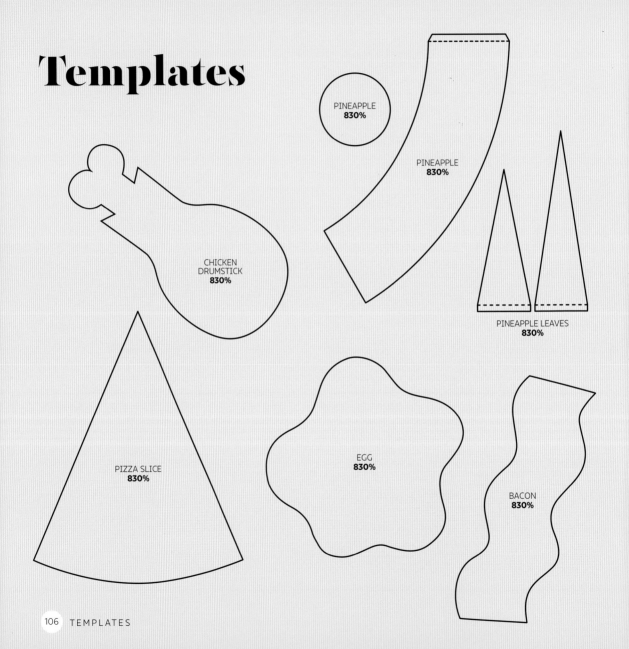

PINEAPPLE
830%

PINEAPPLE
830%

CHICKEN
DRUMSTICK
830%

PINEAPPLE LEAVES
830%

PIZZA SLICE
830%

EGG
830%

BACON
830%

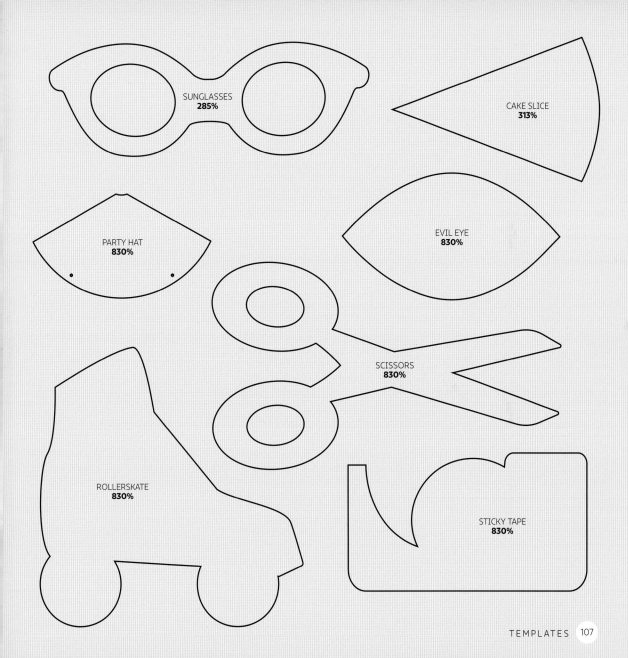

SUNGLASSES
285%

CAKE SLICE
313%

PARTY HAT
830%

EVIL EYE
830%

SCISSORS
830%

ROLLERSKATE
830%

STICKY TAPE
830%

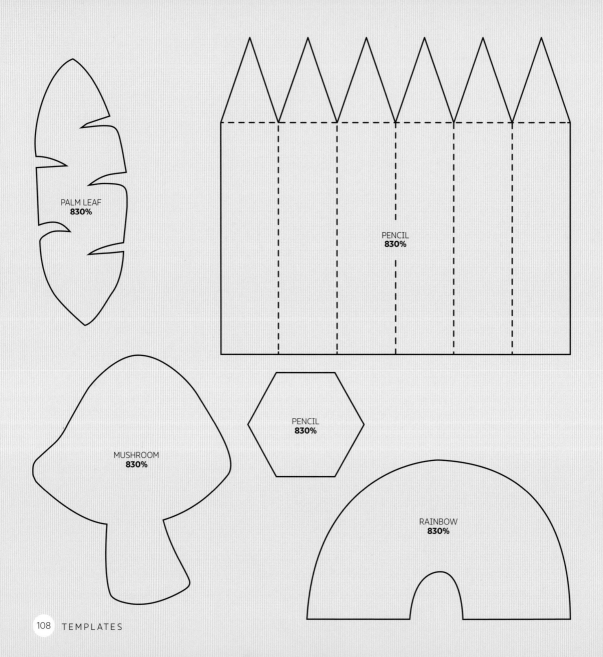

PALM LEAF
830%

PENCIL
830%

MUSHROOM
830%

PENCIL
830%

RAINBOW
830%

MOON
830%

STAR
830%

CRYSTAL
830%

FLORAL
CAKE TOPPERS
483%

CRYSTAL
830%

PEACE SIGN
(FRINGED HANGING DECORATION)
830%

TIKI INVITE
254%

Thank you!

I've wanted to be an author since I was 11 years old, so to be writing the acknowledgements for my very own book is a crazy feeling!

I'd like to thank the following legends:

First and foremost, to my amazing photographer Mark, the perfect partner in crime for this project. Working with you has been a dream and I couldn't have wished for a better person to bring my wacky visions to life!

To my book team: Andrea, Melissa, Erika, Kim, Mark C, Meelee and Muzd — it's been unreal working on this with you.

To the beautiful people who graced the pages of this book and let me force them into all sorts of ridiculous poses for the sake of piñata art: Alicia, Anders, Brooke, Clare, Dan, Esther, Justin, Katie, Mark, Mel, Steph, Tina and Yve — you brought this all to life!

To Clare, Mel and Kara for the many hours you spent helping me construct and decorate all the projects for this book. I literally couldn't have made them all (and probably would have had a meltdown) without you.

To Alex from Sherwood North Catering for the epic cake.

To my family and my amazing boyfriend Matt for supporting me through this project, and all my crazy endeavours.

To everyone who has supported my craft-based design practice over the years, from following along on Instagram, to reading my blog, visiting my market stalls and buying my wares online. It feels so good to be part of such a creative community and I am so appreciative that you guys dig my stuff.

Finally, a big thanks to you for buying/ borrowing this book! I'm so stoked that you took the time to read it and try out the projects, and I hope you are now inspired to create the most fantastic and fun-filled parties ever!

About the author

Kitiya Palaskas is an Australian craft-based designer with a multi-faceted practice specialising in prop, costume and installation design, set dressing, art direction and styling. Her work centres around re-imagining handmade techniques and traditional craft methods in contemporary ways, and is characterised by its bold colours, humorous themes and kitsch, nostalgic nature.

A lifelong passion for making her own party decorations and a love for traditional Mexican handicrafts sparked Kitiya to try her hand at making her own piñatas, and sharing them on her blog. After creating her first ever piñata (a pineapple), her designs expanded to include more tropical fruit, as well as themed shapes for holidays and special occasions, and quirky, everyday objects.

Alongside her design work, Kitiya hosts regular craft workshops, works on a variety of piñata commissions and creates DIY projects and piñata how-tos for magazines and blogs around the world. This is her first book.

kitiyapalaskas.com

Published in 2017 by Hardie Grant Books,
an imprint of Hardie Grant Publishing

Hardie Grant Books (Melbourne)
Building 1, 658 Church Street
Richmond, Victoria 3121
hardiegrantbooks.com

Hardie Grant Books (London)
5th & 6th Floors
52–54 Southwark Street
London SE1 1UN
hardiegrantbooks.com

A Cataloguing-in-Publication entry is available
from the catalogue of the National Library of
Australia at www.nla.gov.au

Piñata Party
ISBN 978 1 74117 529 5

Commissioning Editor: Melissa Kayser
Managing Editor: Marg Bowman
Project Editors: Andrea O'Connor
    & Meelee Soorkia
Editor: Kim Rowney
Design Manager: Mark Campbell
Design and colour reproduction: Erika Budiman
Illustrator: Kitiya Palaskas
Photographer: Mark Lobo
Production Manager: Todd Rechner
Production Coordinator: Rebecca Bryson

Printed in China by 1010 Printing International
Limited